I0203339

The Mysteries of the Revelation No-More

Even a baby can understand them

Amos L. Horton Jr.

Table of Contents

7 above are listed the books that follow

References: Includes all scriptures from the Book Of Revelation (KJV) Series of study on Asia use of internet references "The world of Asia" Greek, Hebrew Dictionary, NKJ, NIV, Nations of the world, Prophetic Manual Vol.1, Asia Internet Usage Stats and Population Statistics, Asia - Wikipedia, the free encyclopedia, Dakes study bible, Quotes from Great Bible Intellectuals, prayer and consecration

Amos Horton Ministries Inc.
P.O. Box 7320
Beaumont Texas 77726

The honorable Bishop Amos L. Horton Jr., was born in Angelina County in 1979 but later his parents moved to Beaumont, TX. As said "like father like son." He proudly states that although he will forever strive he will never be greater that his dad Pastor Amos L Horton Sr. He has never challenged his dad's authority and serves him with all his might. Quoting the bishop, "Dad still is and will always be my most favorite preacher and I hope to walk on his level someday."

I will forever walk in his shadow and that doesn't worry me. I am honored to be number two. Step by step and day by day I long to make daddy proud. Amos Jr, became a second generation preacher by age nine he formerly answered the call to preach the gospel of peace.

He would boldly proclaim the gospel while tears streamed down his face. As a result of this, he quickly became known as the weeping prophet. By age fifteen he was ordained a national evangelist traveling regions beyond the state of Texas preaching the life changing gospel of Jesus Christ. It was said that his wisdom was beyond his years and his level of anointing unexplainable.

By age seventeen he founded (TFC) Teens for Christ which became a very popular organization during his high school years. It was established as an extra-curricular activity all his years in school. TFC caught the eyes of television and the Gospel of Jesus Christ spread abroad. Central Sr. High will always be remembered as the school that respected God because they allowed such a move. The campus became a Harvest field for the kingdom of God and Bishop Amos Horton Jr. The seventeen year old fathered such an experience. He dedicated his life to preaching, excelling in the gifts of the spirit. His first pastoral experience came at age nineteen in Lake Charles, LA. He pastored for one year under the leadership of Bishop McKinley August, Jr. who he still believes God used to make him the caliber of preacher he is today. By the age of twenty, he was traveling the globe far and near preaching the Gospel of Jesus Christ.

Bishop Horton has never been interested in the methodology of denomination and religious philosophy toward the gospel, but rather sought to see souls saved and lives changed.

He believes that true preaching transcends doctrinal barriers and salvation has no prejudice toward denomination. Having a very powerful and mysterious ministry he was given the name "Mystery" in the year 1990. He has been deemed as a "preacher among scribes, he who carries the oracles of God."

It was in the year of 1998 that he brought together an array of extraordinary preachers and founded the Horsemen, a fellowship that spins from C.O.R.E Ministries. Receiving several licenses into various positions somewhat explains his electrifying sermons, that touches the heart of mankind and yet so mesmerizing the souls of men were pierced. He was honored as Lamar University's C.O.P's great orator. His ministry has now been sent to the nations and to the world. The man of God soon developed a heart for leaders taking on his next assignment developing leadership. Pastors and leaders throughout the United States entreated bishop on the basis of church growth and leadership development.

In the year 2008, on the (13th) thirteenth day of just (3) three days before his (29th) twenty-ninth birthday. Bishop Horton was consecrated/affirmed into the office of Bishop. It was a time span of about (7) seven years that he refused this office wanting to make sure that it was indeed God's timing before moving into this position. God has blessed him with a powerful team of bishops who sit on his board embracing the liberty that flows in his vision. In the year 2010 Bishop begin to seek out a covering not just a covering of apostolic power but of apostolic holiness. God then lead him to Apostle Jerry E. Haynes. He is a most excellent covering that has brought a divine order to our bishop's life and ministry. Growing up with strict philosophical doctrines and religiosities that held men captive within an organization bishop has been freed into true religious conviction.

This opens a door of escape from sin for all persons that will walk through this door. He believes that Jesus Christ is the only way into eternal life and does not deviate from the principals of the scriptures. Bishop did not sign up to be popular but he will bring revival in any service.

He is the founder of C.O.R.E. Ministries (Cathedral of Restoration and Evangelism) where his assignment on earth is to restore the body of Christ back to God. He also founded T.O.A (Table of Apostle) an organization that links bishops, apostles, and churches all over the world. He has a true compassion for God's people and wants them to know that all can be restored.

Following in the footsteps of his father Pastor Amos L Horton Sr., he adapted a philosophical, theological, etymological and analytical approach to preaching that has captured the attention of people throughout the United States and the world. Amos Horton Ministries is established on biblical doctrine. Cathedral of Restoration/Evangelism (CORE) and Bishop Amos Horton Jr. seek to be the water of the world that those thirsty may drink and be restored. Founded upon biblical principles, C.O.R.E. focuses on improving our communities, our nation and our world, fulfilled spiritually, economically and emotional given both spiritual and self-satisfaction.

The very heartbeat of C.O.R.E is the Gospel and service to mankind manifest through the spirit of excellence. As a ministry, C.O.R.E. makes no claim to cross every T and dot every I, but strives to do so. Bishop Horton instilled into C.O.R.E. that expressing integrity and compassion to all mankind is an absolute. As an organization, C.O.R.E. does not argue logic, but simply trust God.

Bishop Horton leads this great organization with the love of Christ that this gospel may infiltrate into the local environment, community and proliferate into our nation and the entire world. C.O.R.E. is renowned for being a soul winner and bringing healing to the broken hearted. The vision given to Bishop Horton is that people are restored within and outside of the church walls. Honesty is the foundation of this ministry bringing service to mankind with a proper sense of pride and self-respect. C.O.R.E has been recognized across the nation for its sincerity toward physical and spiritual excellence. This empowers people to have peace within them-selves even if sometimes situations grow worse instead of better.

Bishop Horton is a loud sounding voice throughout the nation that is empowering, mentoring, and supporting spiritual leaders.

As a spiritual father to over 114 churches 307 grandson and granddaughter churches and 147 network churches. Bishop Horton often tells his sons and daughters that they have been molded by God "built with pride and bound for glory." This applies to all mankind and this is what he strives to share with others. As an author his written words are just as effective as his spoken words. Prophet Horton's first book was released in 2007. As a bishop his arms extend various places such as Texas, Arkansas, Virginia, South Carolina, Savannah GA, Ohio, Louisiana and Liberia, Africa and The Bahamas. He has preached before thousands yet maintains a God given humility that illuminates from his spirit. To know Prophet Amos Horton Jr. is to know he stayed with the faith. Embracing the freedom that comes only through Jesus Christ this has separated his ministry from so many others.

There were a lot of complications throughout this walk, but all things worked for the good. Prophet say's "To my Conrad's in the gospel; young men and ladies who have not compromised, we haven't won every battle, but we have ultimately won the war. My life has been filled with so many joys, yet accompanied by so many sorrows. I was in the city of Little Rock (Arkansas) and I was asked this question, "if you could change anything in your life what would it be?" I thought about the good, the bad, the victories and the defeats, my strengths and my weaknesses, then I answered; I would change nothing. It was the combination of everything intermingling together that made me who I am. Who am I God's man?" There is a mandate on his life, it is a global release to take the gospel of Christ to the world.

To pray that the sick be healed, the blind receive sight, those bound be delivered, and that souls would continue to be saved. The heart of this man is to feed the hungry and supply housing for the homeless.

His responsibility is to impact the nation through Christ bringing improvement to individual communities seeing the lives of people change for the better. There will be a day when the world will be taking for Christ and the kingdom advanced bishop wants to play my role in doing so. On August 1, 2010 bishop received his Doctrines Degree from Light of the World Redeem Bible College in Pittsburgh Pennsylvania. Along with his degree is an array of certifications. Certificated in (CIS) Communities in School where he counseled the youth of Texas.

He's a professor in the state of Texas for many local Theological schools in the golden triangle. Certificated into every office of the five-fold he has been deemed a true leader. The oil on his life is that of deliverance, healing and miracles along with the prophetic. He has been proven as a prophet demonstrating all the works of the five-fold was affirmed as Apostle in the year 2011. Bishop is the proud Founder of Cathedral of Restoration/Evangelism, Table of Apostle, The Horseman and also the newly founded League of Extraordinary Ladies and Gentlemen.

Chapter 1: Are You A Member Of That Church

We are often so hypnotized by the mysteries of God's mind that are revealed through the Holy Scriptures. He was and is still a mystery and the most incredible being of all time. He is so secretive yet so revealed, so meek yet so dominate. There is no other name as majestic his name "Jesus" and nothing living or dead, of matter or non-matter can possibly be labeled as his equal. Truly he is in a category all by himself. The suspense of his person creates in the human mind an appetite to search out a higher power. However it is Satan that pollutes mankind with the appalling scheme of false religion. Here lies some of the greatest mysteries that mankind will ever have the privilege to discover. It is here that the mysteries shall be made plain.

[1] The Revelation of Jesus Christ, which God gave unto him, to shew unto his servants things which must shortly come to pass; and he sent and signified it by his angel unto his servant John:

John the apostle being one of the twelve within the circle of Jesus was chosen to witness this vision and revelation from Jesus Christ. He was the only remaining apostle that had a personal relationship with Jesus when he wrote and sent this book to the seven churches. The word Revelation here expresses what it means to be exposed. Its etymology comes from a Greek word apokalupsis translated in other languages to mean apocalypse. By definition this Greek terminology means to uncover; as to raise a curtain so that what waits behind it may be revealed to all those who wait at the curtain to see.

The significance is credited to Jesus who explains the revelation, for it was his assignment to John. He is the one who raises the curtain and his agenda is to reveal the most mystifying and miraculous secrets divulging the precise truths of his return. He not only raises the curtain but he somewhat demands the preacher to share these mysteries with the church. Most who read The Revelation are dumbfounded at its conjectural or almost imaginary delivery. It is a book of symbolism and everything that exists in this book identifies what is to come.

Remember that The Revelation is not predominantly about Jesus Christ, but it is Jesus Christ revelation from God, which he shares with the angel who shares it with John and John's declaration to the seven churches of Asia. It is also in verse one (1) that we discover once again the truths of the trinity for God himself gave the revelation to Jesus Christ.

We will never truly understand the trinity given all our days how God can split himself; even the greatest minds are left to wonder. It is this topic that generates division between many of our churches today. I will write the book revealing even this mystery in God's time. The Revelation was written to explain the mysteries of the lion's return. It is in the Greek word apokalupsis that we see God's desire to reveal himself to mankind. All of the mysteries of what was, what is, and what is to come are revealed in The Revelation. The warning is stern for he mentions that the mysteries of The Revelation would come to pass shortly. The Greek word is tachos it means in this particular book (Revelation) that God will perform these thing immediately. Its literal meaning is swiftly or quickly.

The Revelation is a book of symbolisms however the word signified in verse one (1) denotes that every symbol will and must be revealed. The Greek word for signified or signify is semaino and it literally means to point out and explain. *[2] Who bare record of the word of God, and of the testimony of Jesus Christ, and of all things that he saw.* This is amazing because as the scripture says he has begun to show the mysteries of his mind. The scripture makes it plain in every aspect of life. Jesus Christ stratagem to do the same with the Apostle John. *[3] Blessed is he that readeth, and they that hear the words of this prophecy, and keep those things which are written therein: for the time is at hand.* Again everyone is encouraged to stand at the curtain if they have a desire to see the mysteries that are to come. The promise is that if you hear and receive this prophecy you will be blessed.

It is an angel, which speaks with John eager to share with him the revelation from Jesus that came by God. The angel moves in the spirit of the prophet. He comes with a direct word from God himself. True prophets have a divine message that generates divine change.

He (the angel) proclaims boldly to John in verse four (4). *[4] John to the seven churches which are in Asia: Grace be unto you, and peace, from him which is, and which was, and which is to come; and from the seven Spirits which are before his throne;* Surely you feel the enthusiasm as the angel of the lord begins to declare the mysteries of God's mind in pertinence to the seven (7) churches in Asia.

These warnings are from the mouth of Jesus himself. He is that which is; meaning the only true and living God that exist today. There is no other God besides him.

Any other man, beast, woman, or demon that solicits worship can only be classified as an idol or a false god, for he is that which is. He and only he exist as and is God. He is also that which was, Elohim (Hebrew word or title) the God who started it all. He is not just the God in creation, he is the God of creation and out of him precede the Cosmos, or the entire world (social system). He created the heavens, the earth, and all that dwell therein. (*Gen. Chapters 1 and 2*) *He came into his own, all by himself. His powers unmatchable to anyone else.*

His wisdom so profound he leaves you amazed. He was called by Enoch the Ancient one of days. He is also called the first and the last. He stood there laughing in the dateless past. He created the birds, the beast and the bees. He landscaped the mountains and dug out the seas. He brought balance to both wrong as well as right. He divided the day from the night. When the Cosmos was disordered a major disaster. He brought unity and peace the lord our sovereign master. When the world had no order and reality didn't exist there stood an all conclusive God in the midst. When the wind did not know how to blow and the grass did not know how to grow. When the sun was ignorant to light and the darkness was confused by night. When heat made nothing sweat and water made nothing wet there live a God by the name of Jehovah Elohim. (Self-existing eternal creator)Sitting in the grangers of heaven did Jehovah Elohim writing the blue prints did Jesus whom dwelled in him. When the plan was complete they began to boast and passed the instructions to the Holy Ghost. (See complete book of poems The Mind of a Thinker) **He is that which was, the God that existed before anything. Lastly he is that which is to come.**

This "The Revelation" is such an amazing book pointing out the secrets of God's person along with his Kingdom. That which is, that which was and that which is to come explains God and the way he revealed himself to mankind. That which was, defines the logos (Grk) this was God in heaven in sprit form in a dateless past before being revealed in the person of Jesus Christ. That which is, explains Jesus (Grk) "manna" or Jehovah incarnate whom came into the world to save us and send the comforter who today still is. The dateless past is a period that existed before time a place not subjected to death it is the place of the eternal king, the God of all gods. He who dwells in the dateless past is eternal and there is no time in eternity. (Prophetic Manual Vol. 1/work book available)

When that which is becomes that which was rather when God became incarnate in the person of Jesus Christ, eternity for the first time involves itself with time. Immortality intermingles with mortality and life intermingles with death. It is here that we find the incarnate God put upon a cross because time cannot function with eternity.

Thus derives the (Grk) Kata Lambano or "The Power of the Resurrection." Eternity could not and would not be captured by death even if it was under the jurisdiction of time. It was impossible for the God of the dateless past translated to mean the ancient one of days or the one who existed before days began to die, for in him there is no death at all. The immortal God cages himself in a uniform of contaminated tissue that struggled against his divinity.

This makes him sensitive to time, but not dominated by time, and the forces of eternity that rebelled against God (Satan 1/3 of the angels) could not relate to such power. How that eternal life could exist in mortal flesh insulting the realities of the law designed by God himself. If God put these laws into accomplishment how could they not govern even him? The answer is because he's sovereign meaning he can do what he wants, how he wants, where he wants, when he wants and no one can do anything about it. This is the reason that the creatures of heaven worship him. He is not only the God in life he is the God of life.

It is impossible for him to fail. He did not create the law and government of all things so he could manipulate them but by him does all things consist.

Colossians 1:17 *And he is before all things, and by him all things consist.* If God thinks a thing the law, government and even reality changes with his thought St John 1: 4-5 *In him was life; and the life was the light of men. And the light shineth in darkness; and the darkness comprehended it not.* It is in St. John 1: 1-14 that we read of the manifestation of the incarnate God and understand the power of his person. *In the beginning was the Word, and the Word was with God, and the Word was God. The same was in the beginning with God. All things were made by him; and without him was not anything made that was made. In him was life; and the life was the light of men. And the light shineth in darkness; and the darkness comprehended it not. There was a man sent from God, whose name was John.*

The same came for a witness, to bear witness of the Light, that all men through him might believe. He was not that Light, but was sent to bear witness of that Light.

That was the true Light, which lighteth every man that cometh into the world. He was in the world, and the world was made by him, and the world knew him not. He came unto his own, and his own received him not. But as many as received him, to them gave he power to become the sons of God, even to them that believe on his name: Which were born, not of blood, nor of the will of the flesh, nor of the will of man, but of God. And the Word was made flesh, and dwelt among us, (and we beheld his glory, the glory as of the only begotten of the Father,) full of grace and truth. **Lastly which is to come explains Jesus in his return to the earth to judge both the quick and the dead. The God that cannot until that great day of judgment be defined.**

1st Peter 4:5 *Who shall give account to him that is ready to judge the quick and the dead.*

He left a lamb in a world of wolves, but will return a lion in a world of lambs. Notice God's Strategy; he greets the churches with grace. Even though many of these churches were infested with sin his passion is to warn them so that they would not be victims of his wrath.

Remember warning manifest through pride and pride comes before destruction Proverbs 16:18 *Pride goeth before destruction, and an haughty spirit before a fall.* The word grace in the Greek is charis and it is translated to mean unmerited favor, unmerited meaning divine and favor meaning assistance. The word divine denotes Jesus himself; for he is the only divine one. The word assistance denotes favor so the full translation is to be assisted by a divine Jesus who favors you.

He is simply saying to the churches that I am here to help you combat the plagues of society and if you comply with my admonition you will avoid all the destructions to come.

Many great preachers use The Revelation as an instrument that ignites fear, but there is so much grace and concern from Jesus himself in this powerful book of mystery. Although he would judge their sins he would attempt first to set them free and if the churches would repent and turn they would prohibit to themselves the judgment upon sin.

Furthermore the angel proclaims that the message is also from the seven spirits that are before God's throne. The seven spirits are mentioned throughout The Revelation, but they are never defined.

In verses 1:4, 3:1, 4:5 and 5:6. It makes absolutely no sense to create identities of these seven spirits so I'll waste no time being too theological. Revelation 1:4 explains that the seven spirits are before God's throne. This could imply that these spirits are messengers and they await instructions. As a child I always thought that they were the seven personalities of God, only a childhood ideology. Revelation 3:1 implies that Jesus Christ has or possesses the seven spirits of God. This identifies his authority over them meaning that they are at his command at all times. Revelation 4:5 connects the seven spirits of God with the seven burning lamps that are before God's throne.

This could also mean that the seven spirits have the capacity to bring light in dark places. Finally in Revelation 5:6 the seven spirits are associated with seven eyes.

This could be translated to mean those who have the capacity or ability to see much or to see all. Whichever way we look at it they are a part of God himself and if anything the seven spirits possess seven eyes to watch over the seven churches. Although it is not mention we can perceive that the seven spirits are in some way connected with the person of God and play a key role in the return of Jesus Christ as well as a key role with the seven churches. Notice the area that Jesus targets was Asia; for this was the area where the seven churches were built. (all below underlined information on Asia can be found in direct order from Wikipedia, the free encyclopedia information given to enhance knowledge of Asia all information is underlined above) Asia is the world's prevalent and most heavily populated continent.

It covers 8.6% of the Earth's total surface area (or 29.4% of its land area) and, with over 4 billion people, it contains more than 60% of the world's current human population.

Chiefly in the eastern and northern hemispheres, Asia is traditionally defined as part of the landmass of Eurasia with the western portion of the latter occupied by Europe lying east of the Suez Canal, east of the Ural Mountains and south of the Caucasus Mountains and the Caspian and Black Seas. It is bounded on the east by the Pacific Ocean, on the south by the Indian Ocean, and on the north by the Arctic Ocean. Given its size and diversity, Asia a toponym dating back to classical antiquity is more a cultural concept incorporating a number of regions and peoples than a homogeneous physical entity.

The etymology of Asia originated from the Ancient Greek word "Ασία", first attributed to Herodotus (about 440 BC) in reference to Anatolia or, for the purposes of describing the Persian Wars, to the Persian Empire, in contrast to Greece and Egypt. Herodotus comments that he is puzzled as to why three women names are used to describe one enormous and substantial land mass (Europa, Asia, and Libya, referring to Africa), stating that most Greeks assumed that Asia was named after the wife of Prometheus, but that the Lydians say it was named after

Asias, son of Cotys who passed the name on to a tribe in Sardis. Even before Herodotus, Homer knew of a Trojan ally named Asios and elsewhere he describes a marsh as ασιος (Iliad 2, 461).

The Greek language term may be derived from Assuwa, a 14th century BC confederation of states in Western Anatolia. Hittite *assu*-"good" is probably an element in that name. Alternatively, the etymology of the term may be from the Akkadian word *(w)aṣû(m)*, which means "to go outside" or "to ascend", referring to the direction of the sun at sunrise in the Middle East, and also likely connected with the Phoenician word *asa* meaning east. This may be contrasted to a similar etymology proposed for *Europe*, as being from Akkadian *erēbu(m)* "to enter" or "set" (of the sun). However, this etymology is considered doubtful, because it does not explain how the term "Asia" first came to be associated with Anatolia, which is *west* of the Semitic-speaking areas, unless they refer to the viewpoint of a Phoenician sailor sailing through the straits between the Mediterranean Sea and the Black Sea.

–

It is interesting to note, in Icelandic Saga, ancient Teutons separated Asia from Europe by the river Tanakvisl (or Vanakvisl), which flows into the Black Sea. Eastward across the River (in Asia), so legend tells, was a land known as Asaheim or Asaland, where dwelt Odin, chief god, in his citadel named Asgard.[4] However, *Aesir* and all its forms are related to Sanskrit *asura* and Avestan *ahura*, the local reflexes of the name of a class of divine beings. Asia is also a place filled with demonic and false religion.

Asian philosophical traditions originated in India and China and cover a large spectrum of philosophical thoughts and writings. Indian philosophy includes Hindu philosophy and Buddhist philosophy. They include elements of nonmaterial pursuits, whereas another school of thought from India, Cārvāka, preached the enjoyment of material world.

Also Methidistism and protestism is popular among Koreans Abrahamic religions of Judaism, Christianity and Islam originated in West Asia.

The world's largest Muslim community (within the bounds of one nation) is in Indonesia. South Asia (mainly Pakistan, India and Bangladesh) holds 30% of Muslims.

There are also significant Muslim populations in China, Iran, Malaysia, the Philippines, Russia and most of West Asia and Central Asia. In the Philippines and East Timor, Roman Catholicism is the predominant religion; it was introduced by the Spaniards and the Portuguese, respectively. In Armenia, Eastern Orthodoxy is the predominant religion. Various Christian denominations have adherents in portions of the Middle East, as well as China and India.

Judaism, one of the smaller yet oldest of the Abrahamic faiths, is practiced primarily in Israel (which has either the largest or second largest Jewish population in the world), though small communities exist in other countries, such as the Bene Israel in India. The Indian religions of Sikhism, Hinduism, Buddhism and Jainism originated in South Asia. In East Asia, particularly in China and Japan, Confucianism, Taoism, Zen Buddhism and Shinto took shape.

During the 20th century, in the two most
populous countries of Asia, two
dramatically different political
philosophies took shape. Gandhi gave a
new meaning to Ahinsa, and redefined the
concepts of nonviolence and
nonresistance. Other religions of Asia
include the Zoroastrianism, Shamanism
practiced in Iran and Siberia respectively,
and Animism practiced in the eastern
parts of the Indian subcontinent and in
Southeast Asia. (all above underlined
information on Asia can be found in
direct order from Wikipedia, the free
encyclopedia information given to
enhance knowledge of Asia all
information is underlined above) It was
Asia that would ignite a flame in the
Apostle Paul for it was there that he saw a
place and a people who needed great
deliverance.

The journey begins with Paul and
Barnabus who set out from Antioch Acts
13:4. *So they, being sent forth by the Holy
Ghost, departed unto Seleucia; and from
thence they sailed to Cyprus.* The scripture
states that they abode there for a long
time. Acts 14:28 *And there they abode long
time with the disciples.*

It is here that the book of The Revelation is embossed, so mysterious that it draws the attention of every religion.

So complicated that it cannot be falsely philosophized, yet so simple that even a baby can understand. It is a book that is only comprehended when one has study many if not all of the Holy Scriptures. *[5] And from Jesus Christ, who is the faithful witness, and the first begotten of the dead, and the prince of the kings of the earth. Unto him that loved us, and washed us from our sins in his own blood.* John now writes of Jesus Christ as a faithful witness. He is the one that bares no false report. This identifies the biblical truth and sovereign austerity of Jesus and his word, he can and will not lie.

Fundamentally the writer proclaims that God is faithful and will bring to pass all that is declared in The Revelation. Do not think for one instant that The Revelation is a fairytale. All that is written shall shortly come to pass.

The Greek word that defines Jesus as a witness is martus for he is one that can testify as to what he has seen and created.

Philippians 1:8 states *"For God is my record (martus) how greatly I long after you in the bowels of Jesus Christ."* He again states the witness of Jesus in his expression to the Philippians. This is only because whenever Jesus is involved there is a great guarantee on the situation. If God has spoken it everything spoken will and must come to pass. (For more info on witness look at 2 Cor. 6:12, Acts 22:20, 2 Cor. 1:23, Rev 17:6 and 2:13) He is also called in scripture (5) five the first begotten of the dead.

This does not identify Jesus with being just the first born and only begotten of the father, but it does identify with him being the first to die and to be resurrected.

Thus proving the truth of God's power over death by allowing Jesus to partake of the atrocious fruit of death yet to be the first resurrected, making him the first begotten of the dead. Rev. 1:5 *and from Jesus Christ, the faithful witness, the firstborn of the dead, and the ruler of the kings of the earth To Him who loves us and released us from our sins by His blood.* It was the blood of his death that purified and washed us from the stain of sin.

The great king David anticipated this deliverance crying out in Psalms 51:7 *Purge me with hyssop, and I shall be clean; Wash me, and I shall be whiter than snow.* Jesus died the death of the cross and was literally brought back from the dead. Not just resurrected in spirit, but in body.

Luke 24:36-40 *Now as they said these things, Jesus Himself stood in the midst of them, and said to them, "Peace be unto to you." But they were terrified and frightened, and supposed they had seen a spirit. And He said to them, "Why are you troubled? And why do doubts arise in your hearts? Behold My hands and My feet, that it is I Myself. Handle Me and see, for a spirit does not have flesh and bones as you see I have." When He had said this, He showed them His hands and His feet.*

Once again the Greek word Kata Lambano meaning and explaining not only his death, but also the power of his resurrection. He, Jesus, in death backed tracked, reversed to Adam rescuing him from the grave as well as all patriots who died under the law, while maintaining relationship with God either through Aaron and the priestly order or Abraham and the Melchizedek order.

Jesus is also called the prince of the kings of the earth. The Greek word is "archon" meaning that he is not only the Lord of Lords, but also the King of Kings. The Greek word archon is very informative it holds several English translations. It defines a ruler or one that gives commands. It defines a chief or one that gives instruction and wisdom. It defines a chief ruler or one that gives command, instruction and wisdom. Lastly it defines a magistrate or one that is in authority.

(Mark 3:22, Jn 12:31, 1 Cor. 2:6-8, Eph. 2:2, Matt. 9:18, Lk. 18:18, Lk. 8:41 Jn 3:1, Acts 3:17, Rom. 13:3, Lk. 11:15, Jn 12: 42, Lk 12:58) *[6] And hath made us kings and priests unto God and his Father; to him be glory and dominion forever and ever. Amen.* We should be eternally grateful because his mission in The Revelation is to finalize our kingly priesthood as those who represent the Name of Jesus Christ.

We are a royal people chosen of God to sit in the place of Angels and in some cases judge the fallen angels 1 Corinthians 6:3 *Do you not know that we shall judge angels? How much more, things that pertain to this life?*

This is amazing God will allow man to judge angels. *[7] Behold, he cometh with clouds; and every eye shall see him, and they also which pierced him: and all kindred's of the earth shall wail because of him. Even so, Amen.*

 The fact that he comes with clouds only points out that his return will be from the heavens into the earth. Just for one's enhancement there are three levels to heaven. The sky, outer space and the planet where God dwells. (For information on the levels of heaven and much more purchase Prophetic Manual Vol. 1 and workbook by Pastor Amos Horton) Every person who occupies the earth will see him and wail.

Some will wail out of fear others out of joy.

The message that he comes from the clouds and all will see is a bold statement that loudly announces that everyone will recognize him as God.(Rom. 14:11/Philippians 2: 11)

In scripture number (8) eight he boldly proclaims *[8] I am Alpha and Omega, the beginning and the ending, saith the Lord, which is, and which was, and which is to come, the Almighty.*

He now defines himself as the all-conclusive God, better known to us as Jehovah God. The word alpha meaning the huge or gigantic being translated from the Greek to mean titan. This enormous being that existed before anything else. He is so wide that you can't go around him. He is so low that you can go under him.

He is so high that you can't go over him and so solid that you can't go through him. Yes he is as well the Omega, the same gigantic God that not only existed before the world began, but has been here through world's end, before our time and will be here after world's end during our time. The very life that we have is because of God. He is the beginning and the ending. He is life; having power over death, he is the almighty and yes he is the resurrection from death into eternal life. I would farther challenge the permanency of death. Most proclaim that there is nothing after death.

This is the belief of many religions that argue life to be temporary and death to be permanent. The truth of the matter is that through Jesus Christ we have eternal life. The Christian does not fear death.

We are at peace because through having a personal relationship with God we know death to be temporary and life to be permanent. Where one ends up after death is predicated on what he/she did in life before death. *[9] I John, who also am your brother, and companion in tribulation, and in the kingdom and patience of Jesus Christ, was in the isle that is called Patmos, for the word of God, and for the testimony of Jesus Christ.* Notice how John addresses us?

He identifies us as brother/sister in Christ. It is through ones acceptance of Christ that makes him/her a brother/sister to every believer in Christ. It is not the denomination that predicates believers, all who receive him become the sons of God. He also calls us companions, which expresses the intimacy of our relationship with Christ and each other.

This intimacy is not sexual as in many other religions, but an intimacy of our hearts toward God and each other. The way we treat other Christians reflects to the world how we treat God.

The word companion in this scripture (9) nine means in the English translation to be a partaker. Philippians 1:7 *Even as it is meet for me to think this of you all, because I have you in my heart; inasmuch as both in my bonds, and in the defense and confirmation of the gospel, ye all are partakers of my grace.* We as Christians all share the same grace and the same lord so we should treat each other as such. We were all brought into light by grace through the power of the Holy Spirit and the name of Jesus Christ. As a young boy in school we would always say to those close to us that "we are partners from the womb to the tomb."

The only difference with Christians is that we are family in life, death and eternity.

Through good and the bad times, in joy and tribulation. John talks about tribulation in scripture (9) nine his reference is to persecution of all saints.

We endure these things because of Christ; we endure through temptation, fear, poverty, infirmity, and struggles of every sort. We survived diverse temptation, which in the Greek identifies conditions of all kinds. James 1:2-5 *My brethren, count it all joy when ye fall into divers temptations; Knowing this, that the trying of your faith worketh patience. But let patience have her perfect work, that ye may be perfect and entire, wanting nothing. If any of you lack wisdom, let him ask of God, that giveth to all men liberally, and upbraideth not; and it shall be given him.*

With no hindrance Jesus reveals to John the same gospel preached in Philippians. It is through persecution that we become complete saints that walk in the divine power of God the father, God the son, and God the Holy Ghost. The complete power of the Godhead can and will be manifested in us and we shall be as he is because we will look upon him.

1 Corinthians 15:51-58 *Behold, I shew you a mystery; We shall not all sleep, but we shall all be changed, In a moment, in the twinkling of an eye, at the last trump:*

For the trumpet shall sound, and the dead shall be raised incorruptible, and we shall be changed. For this corruptible must put on incorruption, and this mortal must put on immortality. So when this corruptible shall have put on incorruption, and this mortal shall have put on immortality, then shall be brought to pass the saying that is written,

Death is swallowed up in victory. O death, where is thy sting? O grave, where is thy victory? The sting of death is sin; and the strength of sin is the law. But thanks be to God, which giveth us the victory through our Lord Jesus Christ. Therefore, my beloved brethren, be ye stedfast, unmovable, always abounding in the work of the Lord, forasmuch as ye know that your labor is not in vain in the Lord. The Kingdom of God is worth all the persecution, for Christ himself will establish his kingdom on earth in his second coming. (Matt 4:17, 19:24, Rev. 1:6, 9:5, 10:11, 12:10, 20:4-6, 22:5)

The Apostle John receives The Revelation after being caught up or brought into the heavens because of his consecration on the Lord's Day, he was in the spirit.

John was consecrated unto God, his total person was completely unified with the Holy Spirit.

John had been possessed by the Holy Spirit in the person of God. Even as Satan possessed Judas so did the Holy Spirit possess John. Lk. 22:3 *Then entered Satan into Judas surnamed Iscariot, being of the number of the twelve.*

John was in the spirit on the Lord's Day. Notice that the bible mentions no specific day of the week. Which means that every day is the Lord's Day. John does not dignify the day with a name. This discontinues the imprudence that has developed the existing conflict that argues the day of service unto the lord. We should serve the lord at all times and not set aside a day that we as Christians render service unto the lord. God does not concern himself with petty issues like the day a congregation has a church service. His concern is whether we are abiding by the scripture or whether we are in the flesh on his day and every day is his day.

Whatever day of the week you worship so let it be written so let it be done.

He John was on the Isle that was called Patmos, a rocky island filled with volcanos and trees. It was about 600 miles wide and 30 miles S. W. of Samos surrounded by water. (Dakes study bible on size of the island as well as many ref. on the internet during my study on the Island of Patmos) The Romans made it a desolate place for those who were abolished from Rome. The worst of criminals, murderers, rapist, possessed persons, etc. were free to endure on Patmos. This island was divided from Rome by a large body of water while Romans Guards watched at the shores of Rome just in case anyone if possible could escape the island of Patmos.

Many Romans and criminals worship an idle called Poseidon where it was said he walked the island of Patmos. The lava of the volcano's constantly brought death to the island leaving the stench of decaying carcasses. Not to mention that the island was desolate of edible herb fit for human consumption, and the beast that lived on the island were wild meat eating creatures that could rip a human being apart. The practice of cannibalism multiplied on Patmos and many were eaten alive.

It was a civilization for lawless people who had no fear or respect for God.

Shockingly as punishment John was sacrificed to the island of Patmos, his crime was preaching the word of God and testifying of Jesus Christ. Yet it is his consecration to God that brings him divine protection and safety before he had been caught up to receive

The Revelation. *[10] I was in the Spirit on the Lord's day, and heard behind me a great voice, as of a trumpet.*

He heard a great voice that captivated his attention. John's consecration was not of himself, but God consecrated John so that he could see clearly the mysteries of The Revelation. The Hebrew word ra'ah defines God's gifting to flesh to see him bodily. This voice sounds off in the middle of his most catastrophic evils. It is comforting to know that God can speak even in the most forbidding times.

The same voice that created the heavens and earth in Genesis chapters 1 and 2. The same voice that became flesh in St John 1:1-14. The same voice that spoke to Moses at the burning bush in Exodus 3:1-

10. Lastly in Exodus 19:16-19 God told Moses to receive the law by blowing on a trumpet. God's voice is as a loud persuasive noise that mesmerizes all those who wait at the curtain to receive his sayings.

A trumpet has the greatest echo of any instrument and its sounds ride on the earth's vibrations and carries for miles across.

The Apostle John immediately hears and follows into the spirit the sound of the trumpet. *[11] Saying, I am Alpha and Omega, the first and the last: and, What thou seest, write in a book, and send it unto the seven churches which are in Asia; unto Ephesus, and unto Smyrna, and unto Pergamos, and unto Thyatira, and unto Sardis, and unto Philadelphia, and unto Laodicea. [12] And I turned to see the voice that spake with me. And being turned, I saw seven golden candlesticks;* John is now taken into the halls of heaven, the throne room of Jesus Christ, the mind of Jehovah God himself. Notice he turns to see who speaks to him. He is pursuing the voice of God, which lands him into the mysteries of God's mind.

The sight that he sees brought to arrest his own intelligence, his own wisdom and his own education. Regardless as to how anointed he was he became dumbfounded in the presence of God. When one truly gets into the presence of God he becomes nothing and desires only to know his creator. He, John for the first time in his life beheld (7) seven golden candlesticks. These candlesticks were not just gold in color, but gold in substance. The gold color represents the requirement of purity preached from and in the seven churches of Asia. It is God's desire of a holy and God-righteous church.

The substance of gold signifies that the foundation of the church must be pure for it was pure from the beginning of time. It expresses the requirement of holiness, meaning that pure churches will give birth to pure churches.

He shows him gold candlesticks as a mirror image as to how he sees his church. *[13] And in the midst of the seven candlesticks one like unto the Son of man, clothed with a garment down to the foot, and girt about the paps with a golden girdle.*

This particular candlestick represents the church or kingdom of Jesus Christ where he rules forever and ever amen. The terminology likened unto Son of man represents the sovereignty of his kingdom. The word clothed identifies his body in kingly apparel for it reached from his head to his foot. Every king's garment would rest on his shoulders surrounding his neck surpassing his feet and the train of his garment would drag the ground as he walked through his kingdom. (Dan. 10:5, Dan 7:13, Isaiah 6:1,) The Hebrew word shawl; meaning robe. (Look at Jer. 13:22, Lam: 1:9, Neh. 3:5

[15] And his feet like unto fine brass, as if they burned in a furnace; and his voice as the sound of many waters. His feet being as brass represent the stability of his walk for he will not and does not waiver.

Brass is symbolic of stability, having strength and a solid foundation. It also explains the color of his person. Not intentionally stating the color of his nationality, but the word polished in Daniel 10:5-7 defines him as polished brass or as one renewed or as a refreshed man, beautified with his color.

Spot and tainting from his wars with Satan and the forces of darkness had been removed. His stain of sin because of mankind had been erased as the spots on the king's garments are removed.

He was polished and ready to redeem mankind. His voice like many waters defines the power of his words, which leads all to trembling.

The sound of one ocean magnifies the roar of the greatest thunders. Imagine angry waves from the largest seas with the assistance of the greatest winds. Imagine a Tsunami and the bite of its roar. Think of the roars of billions of lions and bears. Think of the sound of an earthquake off the rector scale. Imagine a category five hurricane that has no intention of hesitant-ting. Afterwards combined all these together and multiply them by (x) eternity, you will then understand the voice that John the Apostle heard. *[16] And he had in his right hand seven stars: and out of his mouth went a sharp two-edged sword: and his countenance was as the sun shineth in his strength.*

[17] And when I saw him, I fell at his feet as dead. And he laid his right hand upon me, saying unto me, Fear not; I am the first and the last:

The right hand of God reveals perfect judgment and strength that he executes to and through the pastors of the churches.

The seven stars represents the seven (7) pastors of the seven (7) churches which represent all the churches and pastors of the world today. The two-edged sword proceeding out of his mouth explains the word that he speaks being what touches the personalities and feelings of mankind. It talks to man's tri-colony, his body, spirit, and his soul. Hebrews 4:12 states *For the word of God is quick, and powerful, and sharper than any two-edged sword, piercing even to the dividing asunder of soul and spirit, and of the joints and marrow, and is a discerner of the thoughts and intents of the heart.*

His word has the capacity to change a person from darkness to light as well as the facility to keep them from changing back into darkness from light. In his mouth is the conviction that reminds us. The faith that teaches us.

The provision that increases us. The sanity for our minds. The healing from all diseases. The peace that passes all understanding. Philippians 4:7 states *And the peace of God, which passeth all understanding, shall keep your hearts and minds through Christ Jesus.* This only comes from the sword that's in his mouth.

Unbelievable is the word that describes his continence for it is likened to the sun. Daniel 10:6 says *His body also was like the beryl, and his face as the appearance of lightning, and his eyes as lamps of fire, and his arms and his feet like in color to polished brass, and the voice of his words like the voice of a multitude.* His continence is defined as the brightest of lights; that we call sun or lightning.

No creature on the face of this earth can view lightning face to face without being destroyed. No creature on the face of the earth can touch the sun without being consumed. The lord has to reveal himself through word because mortals cannot live after seeing the actual person of God unless God allows himself to be seen. (ra'ah Hebrew).

That is why the angel shows the vision to John for he could not look upon Jesus Christ of Nazareth, the true and living God. John had been taken in the spirit on the day that is called Gods. Gifted in that day to see what no-other human could see; and live to talk about it. However when he sees the splendor, magnificence and vivacity of God he falls as a dead man. Just a vision of Jesus knocks him to his knees. I truly believe that every knee shall submit and every tongue confess.

For it is written, *As I live, saith the Lord, every knee shall bow to me, and every tongue shall confess to God.* Romans 14:11. This shows that sincere consecration humbles a man, and when he is humbled he worships God. He lays as a dead man or he lays prostrate before the lord. This is a form of repentance. When one truly taps into the presence of God he/she finds true repentance and sanctification. This is not done out of guilt, but out of hope for he who sees the lord sees himself.

Those individual who experience God's presence will search out the sins in their lives repenting until their struggles exist no more.

[18] I am he that liveth, and was dead; and, behold, I am alive for evermore, Amen; and have the keys of hell and of death. He now encounters the splendor of the Messiah's immortal kingship. In the vision Jesus speaks of himself as being him that liveth.

Explaining his life after death and the blessing of eternity that he has the ability to give to all of us as Christians if we serve him. He simply explains the death, the burial and the resurrection on the cross of Calvary, the empty tomb and his power over the grave. He states that he possess the keys of hell and death. This again points out his sovereign power for his powers are limitless. He can do what he wants, when he wants, how he wants and nobody can do anything about it.

He boldly states in Matt: 16: 18-19 the power of his word. Jesus can deal with any demon or any devil that would try and destroy his perfect will in our lives. Notice he combines hell and death signifying that he is the supreme authority and those who will leave death into hell will happen so by his hand. *[19] Write the things which thou hast seen, and the things which are, and the things which shall be hereafter;*

He now commands and unctions the Apostle John to make a written essay of what he says and shows; so that he would be able to successfully minister the word he speaks to the seven churches.

The word that defines write is to make a record meaning that this was also for the churches to come and all the churches of the world. *[20] The mystery of the seven stars which thou sawest in my right hand, and the seven golden candlesticks. The seven stars are the angels of the seven churches: and the seven candlesticks which thou sawest are the seven churches.* Here he speaks of all the mysteries that he had just revealed. The (Grk) word musterion defines these impossible mysteries being made plain. The Apostle John is ordered to share these mysteries with the church. John has been given the greatest mandate as have all preachers.

He is commissioned to share the gospel of Jesus Christ through faith and demonstration.

It is a burdensome responsibility because preachers too feel the callousness of sin and limitation.

John now embarks upon the most difficult action of his life, to make plain the secrets of the mind of Christ. *[1] Unto the angel of the church of Ephesus write; These things saith he that holdeth the seven stars in his right hand, who walketh in the midst of the seven golden candlesticks;* We see the supreme authority of Christ for he gives instruction to John the Apostle as to how he ministers to the church. He holds in his right hand seven stars. The right hand is symbolic of perfect information, judgment and succession.

The seven stars represents the seven messages to the seven churches. These are the messages that are in God's right hand. Not only does he share with the Apostle John The Revelation, but he also shows and explains through vision the meanings of The Revelation. He is the one in the middle of the churches explaining that he will be with the churches at all times going to and fro making sure order, love and victory remains in the house. *[2] I know thy works, and thy labour, and thy patience, and how thou canst not bear them which are evil: and thou hast tried them which say they are apostles, and are not, and hast found them liars:*

[3] And hast borne, and hast patience, and for my name's sake hast laboured, and hast not fainted.[4] Nevertheless I have somewhat against thee, because thou hast left thy first love.[5] Remember therefore from whence thou art fallen, and repent, and do the first works; or else I will come unto thee quickly, and will remove thy candlestick out of his place, except thou repent.[6] But this thou hast, that thou hatest the deeds of the Nicolaitans, which I also hate. [7] He that hath an ear, let him hear what the Spirit saith unto the churches; To him that overcometh will I give to eat of the tree of life, which is in the midst of the paradise of God.

He identifies the Church at Ephesus, as a church consumed by its desire for things. The message was to the angel of the church. This terminology takes the meaning of pastor. He/she alone must feed the sheep all truths. Jesus asked The Apostle Peter the question that would latter impact the church of Ephesus. John 21:15-17 *15 So when they had dined, Jesus saith to Simon Peter, Simon, son of Jonas, lovest thou me more than these? He saith unto him, Yea, Lord; thou knowest that I love thee. He saith unto him, Feed my lambs.*

16 He saith to him again the second time, Simon, son of Jonas, lovest thou me? He saith unto him, Yea, Lord; thou knowest that I love thee. He saith unto him, Feed my sheep. 17 He saith unto him the third time, Simon, son of Jonas, lovest thou me? Peter was grieved because he said unto him the third time, Lovest thou me? And he said unto him, Lord, thou knowest all things; thou knowest that I love thee. Jesus saith unto him, Feed my sheep.

The responsibility is not to build sanctuaries God will do that. The threefold call of the pastor is to feed the sheep. They knew the word and challenged all false doctrines proving the gospel true. Regardless they had lost their relationship with God, forsaken the command to feed the sheep. Forgetting this stunts the church of Ephesus into a building without a God.

More concerned with building a sanctuary and a people to fill it the congregation itself lost touch with God. This filtered over into the new converts and hindered the move of God. They were doing the work, however they were disconnected from the God that giveth life.

So pre-occupied with the business of church that they lost touch of a valuable love relationship with God. Many churches today have become ensnared with this same trap and with confusing reason. (Revelation 2:1-7). Ephesus was the significant capital city of Asia Minor on the Aegean Sea *(The History of Asia)*. Here at the capital it was important to be recognized. All of us want a part in recognition it is in our nature and sometimes we make sacrifices to get it. Ephesus is now known for its massive metropolitan area of arches, antique streets and ruins. It was a tourist attraction. The place where everyone would come to admire and vacate.

Never the less their image became more important than their God. They begin making themselves comfortable. Forgetting the responsibility to the sheep. Many of them had been overtaken with personal issues that landed them into condemnation. The foundation of their problem was that they left their first love. The Lord makes mention of the deeds of the Nicolaitans stating that it is something that he hates.

The scripture says in Acts 20:29. *For I know this, that after my departing shall grievous wolves enter in among you, not sparing the flock.* 20:30 *Also of your own selves shall men arise, speaking perverse things, to draw away disciples after them.* 20:31 *Therefore watch, and remember, that by the space of three years I ceased not to warn every one night and day with tears.*

Paul had been enlightened by God himself of philosophical (Religious Doctrines) teacher who moved in the spirit of a serpent nesting in and out of the church to destroy some. Those who had the capacity to entice with words and demonstration.

These men were students of an ancient sect who had ties to the Gnostic Gospels. The teachings that argued the possibility of human beings having a relationship with God. They were deceived and reprobate full of folly and sedition. I believe they had shaken hands with Satan himself as he taught them all the ways of lies and deception. Thus we have began to understand the Nicolaitans.

Paul's Concern was for the Ephesian church knowing that those who were skilled in and practice rudiments, theologies, black and white magic would enter into the church as <u>wolves in the coats of sheep's</u> (Matt 7:15).

The Nicolaitans were those who practiced all the ways of darkness and took great honor in turning as many as possible from the Gospel of Jesus Christ. The deeds (ways acts or doctrine) of the Nicolaitans filtered from Satan himself. Anyone who followed and believed their teachings were doomed forever and would literally be possessed by Satan. This demon <u>dresses himself as an angel of light</u> (II Cor. 11:14). Satan is like the mist for it comes sometimes without the rain although it is a substance of the rain. Yes Satan can come in the form of light knowing that a <u>little leaven will destroy the entire lump</u> (Galatians 5:9). Many theologians argued that this is not a spirit of Anti-Christ because it combines truth with error, but I disagree.

The Anti-Christ himself will combine both truth and error with the intent to destroy all who believe.

My great grandmother would always tell us "watch out for those who speak with a fork tongue." A lie always sounds better intermingled with the truth. The church at Ephesus was a target to a demon called diabolos (Grk study on the demonic). He is the demon that slanders God in the minds of people. He lies to the individual opening way for them to be deceived by false gospels.

The leader of the Nicolaitans was a man by the name Nicolaus and he was a heretic. Nicolaus taught the ancient ways of Mormonism the sharing of wives and the comfort of fornication and adultery. It was similar to the doctrine of Balaam and Jezebel. These are the spirits of a dead place coming into the earth realm to destroy the people of God but it will not work. We now identify the love that Christ has for his churches. He gives John a word that will call them back to prayer and repentance so that the doctrines of the Nicolaitans would be removed and filtered out of the church at Ephesus. He promises a reward to all at Ephesus if they obeyed. He said that he would allow them to eat from the tree of life which is in the mist of the paradise of God.

The reference has to be to the Garden of Eden where the tree of life was guarded and protected when Adam and Eve were abolished from its splendors (Gen. chapters. 1-4). He speaks now of the gift of immortality for he removed Adam and Eve from the Garden before they could <u>eat of the tree of life and live forever</u> (Gen. 3:22). The word paradise simply explains a place that offers all that satisfied the needs and personalities of individuals. Jesus sends the Apostle John to call them into repentance to keep them from the punishment of his judgment. God is so wonderful to us that he would warn us before punishing us. Ask yourself am I a member of this church.

[8] And unto the angel of the church in Smyrna write; These things saith the first and the last, which was dead, and is alive; [9] I know thy works, and tribulation, and poverty, (but thou art rich) and I know the blasphemy of them which say they are Jews, and are not, but are the synagogue of Satan. [10] Fear none of those things which thou shalt suffer: behold, the devil shall cast some of you into prison, that ye may be tried; and ye shall have tribulation ten days: be thou faithful unto death, and I will give thee a crown of life.

[11] He that hath an ear, let him hear what the Spirit saith unto the churches; He that overcometh shall not be hurt of the second death. <u>Smyrna</u> was the church that endured great persecution.

They suffered poverty and bereavement (<u>Revelation 2:8-11</u>). The location of Smyrna was just north of Ephesus in a prosperous buying and escalating location. Smyrna was known for its harbors along Aegean Sea as well as its commerce and marketplaces. This was a rich city in Turkey called Ismir where Smyrna was suffering poverty. This church had endured great tribulation not wavering, but trusting in the Gospel of Jesus Christ. They suffered poverty because they would not compromise with sects that controlled the Ismir area. Even struggling in finance they held on to their faith. Therefore they were rich in the things of God.

Smyrna refused to yield to the religions who in that time professed Judaism while on the other hand they blasphemed God and were servants of Satan.

Jesus sends a message through John to comfort Smyrna warning them that their suffering would continue because they love him and his word. He farther states that some of them at Smyrna would be falsely accused and place in prison as an attempt to get them to blaspheme the name of Christ. For ten days *(10 is the number of testing and trials)* Satan would torment them through the hands evil and religious men who hated them because they loved God.

The provision of Smyrna was miraculous, for God himself provided for them. The cults and sects did not understand how that the church of Smyrna had no ties to their false beliefs and the ungodly system at that time yet continued to function as a church. Smyrna immediately became the target of all those religions that opposed Jesus Christ. He promises the church of Smyrna that if they would just overcome that he would spare them when he comes as a lion the second time.

Jesus simply points out that this church would endure no suffering when he returns.

12] And to the angel of the church in Pergamos write; These things saith he which hath the sharp sword with two edges; [13] I know thy works, and where thou dwellest, even where Satan's seat is: and thou holdest fast my name, and hast not denied my faith, even in those days wherein Antipas was my faithful martyr, who was slain among you, where Satan dwelleth.[14] But I have a few things against thee, because thou hast there them that hold the doctrine of Balaam, who taught Balac to cast a stumblingblock before the children of Israel, to eat things sacrificed unto idols and to commit fornication. [15] So hast thou also them that hold the doctrine of the Nicolaitans, which thing I hate.[16] Repent; or else I will come unto thee quickly, and will fight against them with the sword of my mouth. [17] He that hath an ear, let him hear what the Spirit saith unto the churches; To him that overcometh will I give to eat of the hidden manna, and will give him a white stone, and in the stone a new name written, which no man knoweth saving he that receiveth it.

Pergamos was considered to be the worldly church. Located on the lands along the Caicus River in Western Turkey. It was one of the major cities in Asia Minor. Pergamos; they had no order and had given to fables plagued by their itching ears. They assorted doctrines mixing the bible with the doctrine of the Gnostics and Nicolaitans. *(mentioned earlier)* This church had totally deviated from the original design and office assigned them. They Welcomed Satan and his philosophies which gave him authority in their church. Satan had his own seat in the church of Pergamos as counselor. He gave men reason instead of Gospel.

This in wonder due to reason was the cause of death for faithful Antipas. He was murdered in the mist of the saints. *(There is a book called the Acts of Antipas that titles him as the bishop of Pergamos.)* Satan taught them the ways of compromise instead of endurance. He taught them satisfaction instead of sanctification. He taught them wrath instead of mercies and lies instead of truth.

Pergamos had the reflection of Christians and would defend the name of Christ but did not see that they were backslidden. These are the methods of the wicked one, it is to destroy inside the church by infiltrating the gospel. Pergamos was full of sin and needed to repent (Rev. 2:12-17). They had become puppets to the doctrine of balaam which practice voodoo and sorcery all sorts of spells designed to hurt the saints.

It was Balac who submitted to this doctrine only to realize it would not work against the true saints of God. With these doctrines comes the spirit of perversion because fornication began to take its monopoly on Pergamos. Giving birth to divorce and ungodly sex, the piercing of sexual organs and wicked actions and imaginations. Jesus loves them so that his message was repent and be set free so that you too can avoid a quick judgment of destruction. He proclaims that if they repent he would give them hidden manna.

The Greek word for hidden is Krupto identifying revelation that no man has received. This would help them to combat their enemies and remain in the will of God.

It is the manna that is kept secret and only God has and knows its dwelling. This manna would show them how to overcome the attacks of Satan against their lives.

Matt. 5:14 *Ye are the light of the world. A city that is set on an hill cannot be hid.* Lk: 18;34 *Who shall not receive manifold more in this present time, and in the world to come life everlasting.* He also stated that he would give the over-comer a white stone.

This is the ancient times was symbolic of victory. He/she who carried a white stone was designated invincible. This defines victory that knows no defeat <u>more than a conqueror through Jesus Christ</u>. (Romans 8:37) Lastly he would give the over-comer a name that only he/she understood. This would be a name of authority in his kingdom. Whenever it would be mentioned it would represent power. Rev. 3:12 *Him that overcometh will I make a pillar in the temple of my God, and he shall go no more out: and I will write upon him the name of my God, and the name of the city of my God, which is new Jerusalem, which cometh down out of heaven from my God:*

And I will write upon him my new name. This name will represent Jesus himself. It is like the soldier who bears the name of his country. This person will bear the name of God. This individual will be given the authority of the name that he/she bares. The fulfillment of power is in that name. Isaiah 62:2 <u>And the Gentiles shall see thy righteousness, and all kings thy glory: and thou shalt be called by a new name, which the mouth of the LORD shall name.</u>

[18] And unto the angel of the church in Thyatira write; These things saith the Son of God, who hath his eyes like unto a flame of fire, and his feet are like fine brass; The eyes like a flame symbolizes one who is feared as a judge.

In this particular scripture it expresses Gods anger. His eyes are on fire expressing the magnitude of his judgment. The brass feet here denotes him as one who's solid in judgment as well as accurate. He cannot and will not be fooled. The fact that the fire was in his eyes explains that he is able to see through all impurity burning away all contamination just to find what's pure.

He was angry with what was going on in the church and wanted to help them gain deliverance from the powers of the wicked one. *[19] I know thy works, and charity, and service, and faith, and thy patience, and thy works; and the last to be more than the first. [20] Notwithstanding I have a few things against thee, because thou sufferest that woman Jezebel, which calleth herself a prophetess, to teach and to seduce my servants to commit fornication, and to eat things sacrificed unto idols. [21] And I gave her space to repent of her fornication; and she repented not.[22] Behold, I will cast her into a bed, and them that commit adultery with her into great tribulation, except they repent of their deeds. [23] And I will kill her children with death; and all the churches shall know that I am he which searcheth the reins and hearts: and I will give unto every one of you according to your works. [24] But unto you I say, and unto the rest in Thyatira, as many as have not this doctrine, and which have not known the depths of Satan, as they speak; I will put upon you none other burden. [25] But that which ye have already hold fast till I come. [26] And he that overcometh, and keepeth my works unto the end, to him will I give power over the nations:*

[27] And he shall rule them with a rod of iron; as the vessels of a potter shall they be broken to shivers: even as I received of my Father.[28] And I will give him the morning star.[29] He that hath an ear, let him hear what the Spirit saith unto the churches.

Thyatira was the false church that followed a seductive prophetess (Rev. 2:18-29). Thyatira is located in western Asia Minor about 42 miles inland from the Aegean Sea. The prehistoric city admire for its materials and pigment trade it is title today as the Turkish city of Akhisar. It is in this land that sex was and is still bought and sold. It was and is a place of sexual persuasion and perversion.

Jesus wants Thyatira to know that he sees all things and that he really wants to set them free. He is persuaded by his passion so intimately that he commends them for the good before identifying the bad. He points out (6) six reasons as to why Thyatira should be commended. The first tribute was the acknowledgment for their works.

They were a hard working church whose zeal and dedication caused them remain focus on the physical needs of the church which is every Christian's responsibility. The second tribute was to charity. The people at the church of Thyatira loved helping other Christian organization as well as helping the homeless, feeding the poor and taking care of the needs of all those within their capacity to help. The third tribute was about their service. The requirement that a church has to the community were fulfilled in Thyatira. They were a church outside of the walls of the sanctuary. These people were sincere in mission and evangelistic work.

This church took on the philosophy that we as believers are also called to the unsaved. The fourth aspect he commends was their faith. They truly trusted In God to provide them all their needs. They did not waiver in their belief in sound doctrine. The fifth accolade was about their patience. They were willing to endure and stand to see all the results of God come to pass.

They were a church that believed that God was able to do exactly what he said.

Lastly he commends them for going above and beyond to win some to Christ. They did not deviate from what they were called to do, to be exact they would strive to always surpass what was done in times past.

One would think that Thyatira had it all together after reading the accolades that were to describe them. However there was a local woman in the community seducing the men at the church. This woman was bold enough to come into the church of Thyatira and began prostituting herself inside the house of God. The insult was really added to injury when she was not corrected or rebuked.

It seemed that the church was doing the work, so they were not workers of iniquity. They were praised for their works.

They were workers in iniquity having a struggle with sexual perversion and desire. Surely marriages were on the rocks in Thyatira. Homes were destroyed and innocent people were damaged. The scripture calls this woman Jezebel. She is not the Jezebel of 1 Kings Chapters 18 and 19 for she had long been deceased.

The point identified a parallel operation of a like spirit. Jezebel has a taste for kings, priest, royalty, men of standard and power. In her grasp she desires control and influence. She is more concerned with what she wants than what others need and she holds within her persuasion the powers of sexual darkness.

Jezebel's tactic into seduction is to play as one who truly knows God. She studies the scriptures using her knowledge as an open door into a position of power.

Being a faithful student of the Gnostics, (earlier mention) she begins to give men reason for error instead of revelation for perfection. Her words are smooth and soothing. Her approach is custom designed for her prey.

Her style is formulated to endure rejection until it submits. She comes with prophesies of good tidings. She could be labeled as the minister of mercy. Out of her mouth comes no correction only compromise and reason. She teaches that God is merciful and that he made man and woman for each other. Her benefit is control, power, money and confusion.

Keep in mind the answer to every man is seduction. If anyone gets caught in her web she will drained them of everything they possess until she totally destroys them. Not only was she seducing men, but she had been given the title of prophetess permitted to teach in the church of Thyatira.

Out of boldness she made sacrifices to idols in the house of God. Leading many into foolish doctrine and lustful spirits. Jesus understands the power of this regenerated Jezebelic philosophy and gives even her time to repent, but she refused. It is Jezebel's character to reject the things of God because her ways or degenerate growing on pride and self-righteousness. Notice what Jesus says "I will cast her into a bed." He is going to turn her over to having a reprobate mind. This allows her to be consumed by her ways and desires.

Whoever lies with her if they don't repent will suffer great tribulation. The casting her into the bed also identifies disease for she will be cast into the bed by sickness and her children will die of deadly diseases.

It is through this that men will understand that God searches the reins, (Gk) (nephros meaning kidneys or the first parts of the fetus) in our language but the innermost mind in other languages. God knows all our secrets so it makes no sense to try and hide from God. 1 John 1:8-10 says *"If we say that we have no sin, we deceive ourselves, and the truth is not in us. If we confess our sins, he is faithful and just to forgive us our sins, and to cleanse us from all unrighteousness. If we say that we have not sinned, we make him a liar, and his word is not in us."* It is God who searches the innermost parts of the heart exposing and delivering any of his children from darkness into light.

[1] And unto the angel of the church in Sardis write; These things saith he that hath the seven Spirits of God, and the seven stars; I know thy works, that thou hast a name that thou livest, and art dead.[2] Be watchful, and strengthen the things which remain, that are ready to die: for I have not found thy works perfect before God.

[3] Remember therefore how thou hast received and heard, and hold fast, and repent. If therefore thou shalt not watch, I will come on thee as a thief, and thou shalt not know what hour I will come upon thee.[4] Thou hast a few names even in Sardis which have not defiled their garments; and they shall walk with me in white: for they are worthy.[5] He that overcometh, the same shall be clothed in white raiment; and I will not blot out his name out of the book of life, but I will confess his name before my Father, and before his angels.[6] He that hath an ear, let him hear what the Spirit saith unto the churches.

Sardis is located on the banks of the Pactolus River in western Asia Minor, 60 miles inland from Ephesus and Smyrna.

It's popular ruins include the decadent temples and bath house complexes. The church titled as "the dead church" a church that slept and missed the blessing. (Revelation 3:1-6). They had a form of Godliness therefore they seemed alive, but they denied the power that brought life. 2 Timothy 3:5 *Having a form of godliness, but denying the power thereof: from such turn away.*

Jesus points out four things pertaining to Sardis. He first mentions works not as a compliment, but to expose their falsehood. People in the community thought that they were a powerful and living church. Maybe they had a good church experience or maybe the choir sang marvelously, but they were dead. It was a church of entertainment and no edification. It's a place of dancing, but no worship, a place of gifts, but no anointing. It's a place of influence, but no power. They could draw the people in, but could not change their lives.

It was just a good church service where only a few had a true relationship with God. This church like some of the others had been confused by the Gnostics. A contaminated doctrine had infiltrated Sardis turning many to compromise instead of holiness. The majority of the church fell asleep while in sin convinced that their sins were only habits that humans or deduce to be involved with. They had been compromised and viewed their sins as the weights of life that easily come upon all mankind thinking that there was no need to change.

Hebrews 12: 1 state: *Wherefore seeing we also are compassed about with so great a cloud of witnesses, let us lay aside every weight, and the sin which doth so easily beset us, and let us run with patience the race that is set before us.*

Even the habit must be laid aside because habits matriculate into strongholds that eventually mature into the office of ruling demons who allow our bodies to maintain a form of godliness while we are filled with godlessness. Jesus then gives five commands to Sardis with the intent of sparing them from the punishments that would come. He says "be watchful" this is advice for them to consider their ways and surroundings. He wants them to see were the enemy was able to enter in. Secondly he says "strengthen thc things that remain." The command to regroup and utilize the strategies that have always worked.

He wants them to go back to the ABC'S of the Gospel "Always Be Consecrated." He wants them to pray and seek his face. He wants them to study the word, and return to the heart of worship.

He then commands that they would remember their teaching, remember the word of God. He wants them to put into action, the principals of the Gospel which destroy all the demonic plots against the kingdom of God. Next he says to Sardis after doing these things don't get discouraged, no matter how long it take to re-establish order it will come to manifestation. II Thess. 3:11-13 *For we hear that there are some which walk among you disorderly, working not at all, but are busybodies. Now them that are such we command and exhort by our Lord Jesus Christ, that with quietness they work, and eat their own bread. But ye, brethren, be not weary in well doing.* In essence not everyone will submit to deliverance, but all those who hunger and thirst after righteousness shall be filled. *"Blessed are they which do hunger and thirst after righteousness: for they shall be filled."*

Matt. 5:6 finally he request that they in the church of Sardis repent. His exhortation is that they turn from their wicked ways and hate that which is ungodly so that they could receive the promise of eternal life. The word repent here means to turn away from things knitted to your heart. (soul ties)

It could have been relationships with family or lovers. Jesus Christ wanted them to be free of this bondage so that he could bless the church of Sardis. It is here that Jesus opens to Sardis the revelation of an ancient scripture that today has becomes the requirement for every Christian. *"If my people, which are called by my name, shall humble themselves, and pray, and seek my face, and turn from their wicked ways; then will I hear from heaven, and will forgive their sin, and will heal their land."*

He was not saying that the church of Sardis had to do this alone, but if they would consecrate their hearts back to God he would free them from the ties that had them bound. Although Jesus had compassion he was aware of the stronghold on the minds of the people. Some of them contemplated continuing in sin so he warns them "I will come as a thief in the night" He does not want to scare the church, but to remind them that Satan plays games and all his games are for keeps. Jesus does not want them to get caught up in the ideal that they have as much time as they needed.

Sardis was filled with youth those who had the mindset that they were still young with a whole life ahead of them. Many of them had issues with youthful lust. They were entangled and in some cases did not want to be free. 2 Timothy 2:22 *Flee also youthful lusts: but follow righteousness, faith, charity, peace, with them that call on the Lord out of a pure heart.* He warns them to practice holiness now! That they would not forfeit the blessings of God.

He points out the few that have not submitted to ungodliness and as a reward they would walk with him in white. To walk with him identifies their worthiness; Jesus feels that these few deserve revelation knowledge and recognition so he would allow them to walk with him.

This is one of the greatest experiences a transformed man can receive. Where Jesus walks has never been discovered by man. He identifies the depths of revelation stating that he would show the few over-comers great and mighty things. Jeremiah 33: 3 states *Call unto me, and I will answer thee, and show thee great and mighty things, which thou knowest not.* The white identifies them being covered by one who is perfect and pure.

Jesus himself will cover them and where he walks they will walk. It is the promise of covenant with man and God for all eternity.

If we would choose righteousness as the few at Sardis, we will be blood covenant partners translated to mean heirs and joint heirs with Jesus Christ.

Romans 8:15-17 *"For ye have not received the spirit of bondage again to fear; but ye have received the Spirit of adoption, whereby we cry, Abba, Father. The Spirit itself beareth witness with our spirit, that we are the children of God: And if children, then heirs; heirs of God, and joint-heirs with Christ; if so be that we suffer with him, that we may be also glorified together."* This same promise is given to those who needed to repent. Thus proving that he Jesus has no respect of persons. Romans 2:11 *"For there is no respect of persons with God."*

He wants the church to be aware that he is serious about his return and his judgment.

Jesus tells them he will not blot them out of the book of life which is man's pass into the kingdom of heaven. Exodus 32:32-33 *"Yet now, if thou wilt forgive their sin--; and if not, blot me, I pray thee, out of thy book which thou hast written. And the LORD said unto Moses, Whosoever hath sinned against me, him will I blot out of my book."* Even as Moses interceded for the people, Jesus says he will confess the names of all who repents before the Father and his angels. Meaning that he can approve their names to remain written. (Psalms 69:25-28, Acts 1:20, Rev 22:18-19.)

He then says in scripture (6) six of chapter (3) three to pay attention and listen to what he says it is for the safety of their lives. *[7] And to the angel of the church in Philadelphia write; These things saith he that is holy, he that is true, he that hath the key of David,*

He that openeth, and no man shutteth; and shutteth, and no man openeth; Philadelphia was the church of brotherly love full of patience and endurance (Revelation 3:7-13). This church is located on the Cogamis River in the western Asia Minor, it's about 80 miles east of Smyrna.

Philadelphia was a very religious quarters known for its variety of temples and worship centers. Notice what is spoken of in pertinence to Philadelphia. Jesus has identified himself as the one that is holy and true. The word holy explains that he is the over-comer of sin and has power over all error. He is flawless and possesses the formula for holiness. There is no sin that exist in him and he is the God without error. The word holiness separates Jesus from all others who have been deemed as gods. Most religions and the philosophies of their leader are based on philosophical doctrines that relate and compromise with human error. This is the reason many follow false religion.

They have a sense of relationship with a higher being while at the same time enjoy the lasciviousness of their own persons. It seems that the world does not want true holiness. Jesus Christ gives us grace to abhor (hate) sin and strength through faith to live without it. He truly wants us to be blameless and to live long prosperous lives because he understands that the wages of sin is death, but the gift of God is eternal life.

Jesus wants all to experience the magnitude of eternity and in-order to do so we must strive to be like him. He is not only holy, but he is also true. The word true explains his sincerity with us and to us because he's sincere about responsibility. He was the lamb slain for the foundation of the word. He became sin so that we could become the righteousness of God.

[8] I know thy works: behold, I have set before thee an open door, and no man can shut it: for thou hast a little strength, and hast kept my word, and hast not denied my name. He points out four justifications for Philadelphia. They are as follows: works, little strength, kept my word, faithful not denying my name. This was a church of action. They worked in building the kingdom not a building or a denomination. They were kingdom minded people operating in their God purpose. They were truly about God's business. Although they had few friends and grew exhausted having a little strength they did not quit. They knew that in their weakness his strength would be made perfect.

II Corinthians 12:9 *And He said to me, "My grace is sufficient for you, for My strength is made perfect in weakness." Therefore most gladly I will rather boast in my infirmities, that the power of Christ may rest upon me.*

When a man fights against his own appetite he/she will experience the power of God that strengthens him/her to resist all temptation and to overcome the strategies of the wicked one. It is true that the church of Philadelphia had weaknesses, but they were fighting to stay in the will of God. They were keepers of the word not compromising the scriptures, but holding fast to the principals of Jesus Christ. They preached Jesus as the only way to eternal life in disregards to their direct challenges of the Gnostics that came through the religion of Islam that had set up camp around them. If we as the Christian churches compromise the Gospel with other religions we have failed and make Jesus Christ death and resurrection of none effect. Lastly they stood for Jesus Christ at all times not ashamed and faithful to the God of all creation.

[9] Behold, I will make them of the synagogue of Satan, which say they are Jews, and are not, but do lie; behold, I will make them to come and worship before thy feet, and to know that I have loved thee. Jesus first declares once again that those who are bound to Satan will and must recognize that he is God. There were many in this time pretending to be Christians, but were filled with lies and deceit. They worship Satan in his synagogue being full of evil thoughts and actions. Jesus says he will make them worship before the feet of them at Philadelphia. He does not mean that he would have the liars worship Philadelphia the church, but that he would cause them to worship him and allow Philadelphia to see it happen. This he would do to prove to Philadelphia that he was with them and he loved them.

He simply says to Philadelphia that I am on your side. *[10] Because thou hast kept the word of my patience, I also will keep thee from the hour of temptation, which shall come upon all the world, to try them that dwell upon the earth.* Philadelphia was the enduring church full of faith and poised.

They were not running to win, but to finish the course that was set before them. They suffered because they were dedicated and would not forfeit the requirement of holiness. Jesus says he will keep them from the hour of temptation.

This is not the hour of temptation that "Daniel 70th week" (future temptation) tribulation, but a time of testing that would be coming in their day. Jesus was going to give them rest in the middle of that temptation. *[11] Behold, I come quickly: hold that fast which thou hast, that no man take thy crown.*

He now identifies with the coming of his kingdom and the day of rapture when the children of God will be caught up and taken with Jesus Christ himself. His warning is that they remain constant not given in to the coming enticement that will manifest before all churches allowing others to steal their crown. The crown represents a place of authority in the kingdom of God. There is reserved seating at all times and a V.I.P into the entire kingdom of Jesus Christ.

[12] Him that overcometh will I make a pillar in the temple of my God, and he shall go no more out: and I will write upon him the name of my God, and the name of the city of my God, which is new Jerusalem, which cometh down out of heaven from my God: and I will write upon him my new name.[13] He that hath an ear, let him hear what the Spirit saith unto the churches.

He farther mentions that to the over-comers he would give them an unmovable office in the kingdom of his God. This identifies the highest of office available to a Christian who enters into eternal life. He the over-comer will talk face to face with the fullness of the Godhead allowed to give instructions in the kingdom. Colossians 2:9 *For in Him dwells all the fullness of the Godhead bodily;* The Godhead explains somewhat the trinity, how that one God reveals himself in three person.

The person of the father, the person of the son and the person of the Holy ghost. Jesus will reveal to the over-comer the mystery of the trinity. The over-comer will also receive the name of God written on him.

Meaning on his garments, like a badge to a uniform also in his mind or spirit. The over-comer will move as God thinks for he will be a part of the mind of God.

Every person in the kingdom of the city of Jerusalem, "the city of God" will note and respect the over-comer for he will wear the name that is above every name as chief in the house of immortality. He mentions of Jerusalem being made new as if the earth will be re-created and re-established as was the garden of Eden **Rev 21:5** *Now I saw a new heaven and a new earth, for the first heaven and the first earth had passed away. Also there was no more sea. Then I, John, saw the holy city, New Jerusalem, coming down out of heaven from God, prepared as a bride adorned for her husband. And I heard a loud voice from heaven saying, "Behold, the tabernacle of God is with men, and He will dwell with them, and they shall be His people. God Himself will be with them and be their God. And God will wipe away every tear from their eyes; there shall be no more death, nor sorrow, nor crying.*

There shall be no more pain, for the former things have passed away."

Then He who sat on the throne said, "Behold, I make all things new." And He said to me, "Write, for these words are true and faithful."

Jesus says he will put also his new name on the over-comer. This would be in the earth that the over-comer would ware the new name of Christ. (Rev. 7:1-8, 14:1, 22:4, 21:2, Chapters 9/10, 24/27, 22:1-3. Finally Jesus reminds the over-comer to listen to what he is saying to his beloved "the church".

[14] And unto the angel of the church of the Laodiceans write; These things saith the Amen, the faithful and true witness, the beginning of the creation of God;
The church of Laodicea was the church caught in between their love for God and their passions for the things of the world.

This particular conflict lands them into a confused state which gave birth to a "lukewarm" church, walking as a double-minded man unstable in all their ways.

James 1:5-8 says *If any of you lack wisdom, let him ask of God, that giveth to all men liberally, and upbraideth not; and it shall be given him.*

*But let him ask in faith, nothing wavering.
For he that wavereth is like a wave of the
sea driven with the wind and tossed. For let
not that man think that he shall receive any
thing of the Lord. A double minded man is
unstable in all his ways.* This church
possessed a faith that was neither hot nor
cold (Rev. 3:14-22). Laodicea is located in
the Lycus River Valley of western Asia
Minor, a primary trade route between the
cultures of the West/East. Laodicea was
known as a primary hub for the Roman
channel system. Located in a prime area
where trade was dependable.

Along with the entering and exiting of
many cultures it was easy to find many
avenues of compromise.

The word written to this church was *[15]
I know thy works, that thou art neither cold
nor hot: I would thou wert cold or hot.[16]
So then because thou art lukewarm, and
neither cold nor hot, I will spew thee out of
my mouth.[17] Because thou sayest, I am
rich, and increased with goods, and have
need of nothing; and knowest not that thou
art wretched, and miserable, and poor, and
blind, and naked:*

Notice in scripture (14) fourteen Jesus calls himself Amen. This defines him as being the uncompromising God full of grace and truth. John 1:10-14 *He was in the world, and the world was made by him, and the world knew him not. He came unto his own, and his own received him not. But as many as received him, to them gave the power to become the sons of God, even to them that believe on his name: Which were born, not of blood, nor of the will of the flesh, nor of the will of man, but of God. And the Word was made flesh, and dwelt among us, (and we beheld his glory, the glory as of the only begotten of the Father,) full of grace and truth.* It also defines him as being the bottom line, the final option, or the last line of defense. Meaning that everything has to go through him. He does not compromise his authority.

He Jesus is truly the God above all Gods. The church of Laodicea was like food that had spoiled on a man's stomach leaving a nauseating feeling. This was the reason Jesus says he would vomit them out of his mouth. This church has an identity crisis seeing themselves as what they were not.

[17] Because thou sayest, I am rich, and increased with goods, and have need of nothing; and knowest not that thou art wretched, and miserable, and poor, and blind, and naked: They were not reprobate only influenced, consumed by the pride of life. They were aware of their true condition, but would rather lie to themselves rather than to be honest with God.

This poverty that Laodicea faced was not only in the area of finance. They were not struggling with money alone, but their physical poverty was the expression of their spiritual poverty. III John 1:2 says *Beloved, I wish above all things that thou mayest prosper and be in health, even as thy soul prospereth.* They were lying to themselves as a result of lying to God. The church that had an image, but no relationship. They were able to fool many in the community, but not God. It was trying to maintain an image that cause them to become miserable.

The Grk word talaiporos meaning to suffer because of dishonesty or to suffer unnecessarily because of something that one brings upon oneself.

[18] I counsel thee to buy of me gold tried in the fire, that thou mayest be rich; and white raiment, that thou mayest be clothed, and that the shame of thy nakedness do not appear; and anoint thine eyes with eyesalve, that thou mayest see. Jesus now reason or negotiates with them although he does not compromise he wants them to be free. The word here is a Greek terminology agoradzo it means to do business with God and only on his terms shall he negotiate. Its literal meaning is to meet at the market place and be prepare to pay the full price. Reason being is because Jesus had already died and negotiated with the father while we were dead to sin being the property of Satan and the children of hell.

However while we were yet sinners Christ died for the ungodly making a deal with God so that we could receive eternal life. Romans 5:6 states *For when we were yet without strength, in due time Christ died for the ungodly.* The deal was already made in heaven between God the father and God the son. Jesus could not allow Laodicea to breech the contract between him and God for the souls of the world.

There is but one option and that is holiness, for holiness without no man see's the lord.

Hebrews 12:14 states *Follow peace with all men, and holiness, without which no man shall see the Lord:* Jesus is firm with his negotiations and determined not to deviate from his agreement with God the father.*[19] As many as I love, I rebuke and chasten: be zealous therefore, and repent.*

[20] Behold, I stand at the door, and knock: if any man hear my voice, and open the door, I will come in to him, and will sup with him, and he with me.

[21] To him that overcometh will I grant to sit with me in my throne, even as I also overcame, and am set down with my Father in his throne.

[22] He that hath an ear, let him hear what the Spirit saith unto the churches. He sends such a strong rebuke and correction to the church of Laodicea because he loves them. He desired for them to enter into his eternal kingdom.

Jesus says that he wants a relationship with them as with all his churches.

That's the reason he stands at the door knocking. Hear my voice and open the door is his plea. I want to come in so don't ignore my warnings.

If the church would but open the door he would come in and sup or engage himself in a life changing relationship that gives access into the kingdom of God.

Lastly he says that if they would overcome they would be allowed to have a seat of power and authority with God the son and God the father sitting as one of the chiefs in the kingdom of God.

Rev.1[1] The Revelation of Jesus Christ, which God gave unto him, to shew unto his servants things which must shortly come to pass; and he sent and signified it by his angel unto his servant John:
[2] Who bare record of the word of God, and of the testimony of Jesus Christ, and of all things that he saw.
[3] Blessed is he that readeth, and they that hear the words of this prophecy, and keep those things which are written therein: for the time is at hand.

[4] John to the seven churches which are in Asia: Grace be unto you, and peace, from him which is, and which was, and which is to come; and from the seven Spirits which are before his throne;

[5] And from Jesus Christ, who is the faithful witness, and the first begotten of the dead, and the prince of the kings of the earth. Unto him that loved us, and washed us from our sins in his own blood,

[6] And hath made us kings and priests unto God and his Father; to him be glory and dominion forever and ever. Amen.

[7] Behold, he cometh with clouds; and every eye shall see him, and they also which pierced him: and all kindred's of the earth shall wail because of him. Even so, Amen.

[8] I am Alpha and Omega, the beginning and the ending, saith the Lord, which is, and which was, and which is to come, the Almighty.

[9] I John, who also am your brother, and companion in tribulation, and in the kingdom and patience of Jesus Christ, was in the isle that is called Patmos, for the word of God, and for the testimony of Jesus Christ.

[10] I was in the Spirit on the Lord's day, and heard behind me a great voice, as of a trumpet.

[11] Saying, I am Alpha and Omega, the first and the last: and, What thou seest, write in a book, and send it unto the seven churches which are in Asia; unto Ephesus, and unto Smyrna, and unto Pergamos, and unto Thyatira, and unto Sardis, and unto Philadelphia, and unto Laodicea.

[12] And I turned to see the voice that spake with me. And being turned, I saw seven golden candlesticks;

[13] And in the midst of the seven candlesticks one like unto the Son of man, clothed with a garment down to the foot, and girt about the paps with a golden girdle.

[14] His head and his hairs were white like wool, as white as snow; and his eyes were as a flame of fire;

[15] And his feet like unto fine brass, as if they burned in a furnace; and his voice as the sound of many waters.

[16] And he had in his right hand seven stars: and out of his mouth went a sharp twoedged sword: and his countenance was as the sun shineth in his strength.

[17] And when I saw him, I fell at his feet as dead. And he laid his right hand upon me, saying unto me, Fear not; I am the first and the last:

[18] I am he that liveth, and was dead; and, behold, I am alive for evermore, Amen; and have the keys of hell and of death.

[19] Write the things which thou hast seen, and the things which are, and the things which shall be hereafter;

[20] The mystery of the seven stars which thou sawest in my right hand, and the seven golden candlesticks. The seven stars are the angels of the seven churches: and the seven candlesticks which thou sawest are the seven churches.

Rev.2[1] Unto the angel of the church of Ephesus write; These things saith he that holdeth the seven stars in his right hand, who walketh in the midst of the seven golden candlesticks;

[2] I know thy works, and thy labour, and thy patience, and how thou canst not bear them which are evil: and thou hast tried them which say they are apostles, and are not, and hast found them liars:

[3] And hast borne, and hast patience, and for my name's sake hast laboured, and hast not fainted.

[4] Nevertheless I have somewhat against thee, because thou hast left thy first love.

[5] Remember therefore from whence thou art fallen, and repent, and do the first works; or else I will come unto thee quickly, and will remove thy candlestick out of his place, except thou repent.

[6] But this thou hast, that thou hatest the deeds of the Nicolaitans, which I also hate.

[7] He that hath an ear, let him hear what the Spirit saith unto the churches; To him that overcometh will I give to eat of the tree of life, which is in the midst of the paradise of God.

[8] And unto the angel of the church in Smyrna write; These things saith the first and the last, which was dead, and is alive;

[9] I know thy works, and tribulation, and poverty, (but thou art rich) and I know the blasphemy of them which say they are Jews, and are not, but are the synagogue of Satan.

[10] Fear none of those things which thou shalt suffer: behold, the devil shall cast some of you into prison, that ye may be tried; and ye shall have tribulation ten days: be thou faithful unto death, and I will give thee a crown of life.

[11] He that hath an ear, let him hear what the Spirit saith unto the churches; He that overcometh shall not be hurt of the second death.

[12] And to the angel of the church in Pergamos write; These things saith he which hath the sharp sword with two edges;

[13] I know thy works, and where thou dwellest, even where Satan's seat is: and thou holdest fast my name, and hast not denied my faith, even in those days wherein Antipas was my faithful martyr, who was slain among you, where Satan dwelleth.

[14] But I have a few things against thee, because thou hast there them that hold the doctrine of Balaam, who taught Balac to cast a stumblingblock before the children of Israel, to eat things sacrificed unto idols, and to commit fornication.

[15] So hast thou also them that hold the doctrine of the Nicolaitans, which thing I hate.

[16] Repent; or else I will come unto thee quickly, and will fight against them with the sword of my mouth.

[17] He that hath an ear, let him hear what the Spirit saith unto the churches; To him that overcometh will I give to eat of the hidden manna, and will give him a white stone, and in the stone a new name written, which no man knoweth saving he that receiveth it.

[18] And unto the angel of the church in Thyatira write; These things saith the Son of God, who hath his eyes like unto a flame of fire, and his feet are like fine brass;

[19] I know thy works, and charity, and service, and faith, and thy patience, and thy works; and the last to be more than the first.

[20] Notwithstanding I have a few things against thee, because thou sufferest that woman Jezebel, which calleth herself a prophetess, to teach and to seduce my servants to commit fornication, and to eat things sacrificed unto idols.

[21] And I gave her space to repent of her fornication; and she repented not.

[22] Behold, I will cast her into a bed, and them that commit adultery with her into great tribulation, except they repent of their deeds.

[23] And I will kill her children with death; and all the churches shall know that I am he which searcheth the reins and hearts: and I will give unto every one of you according to your works.

[24] But unto you I say, and unto the rest in Thyatira, as many as have not this doctrine, and which have not known the depths of Satan, as they speak; I will put upon you none other burden.

[25] But that which ye have already hold fast till I come.

[26] And he that overcometh, and keepeth my works unto the end, to him will I give power over the nations:

[27] And he shall rule them with a rod of iron; as the vessels of a potter shall they be broken to shivers: even as I received of my Father.

[28] And I will give him the morning star.

[29] He that hath an ear, let him hear what the Spirit saith unto the churches.

Rev.3[1] And unto the angel of the church in Sardis write; These things saith he that hath the seven Spirits of God, and the seven stars; I know thy works, that thou hast a name that thou livest, and art dead.

[2] Be watchful, and strengthen the things which remain, that are ready to die: for I have not found thy works perfect before God.

[3] Remember therefore how thou hast received and heard, and hold fast, and repent. If therefore thou shalt not watch, I will come on thee as a thief, and thou shalt not know what hour I will come upon thee.

[4] Thou hast a few names even in Sardis which have not defiled their garments; and they shall walk with me in white: for they are worthy.

[5] He that overcometh, the same shall be clothed in white raiment; and I will not blot out his name out of the book of life, but I will confess his name before my Father, and before his angels.

[6] He that hath an ear, let him hear what the Spirit saith unto the churches.

[7] And to the angel of the church in Philadelphia write; These things saith he that is holy, he that is true, he that hath the key of David, he that openeth, and no man shutteth; and shutteth, and no man openeth;

[8] I know thy works: behold, I have set before thee an open door, and no man can shut it: for thou hast a little strength, and hast kept my word, and hast not denied my name.

[9] Behold, I will make them of the synagogue of Satan, which say they are Jews, and are not, but do lie; behold, I will make them to come and worship before thy feet, and to know that I have loved thee.

[10] Because thou hast kept the word of my patience, I also will keep thee from the hour of temptation, which shall come upon all the world, to try them that dwell upon the earth.

[11] Behold, I come quickly: hold that fast which thou hast, that no man take thy crown.

[12] Him that overcometh will I make a pillar in the temple of my God, and he shall go no more out: and I will write upon him the name of my God, and the name of the city of my God, which is new Jerusalem, which cometh down out of heaven from my God: and I will write upon him my new name.

[13] He that hath an ear, let him hear what the Spirit saith unto the churches.

[14] And unto the angel of the church of the Laodiceans write; These things saith the Amen, the faithful and true witness, the beginning of the creation of God;

[15] I know thy works, that thou art neither cold nor hot: I would thou wert cold or hot.

[16] So then because thou art lukewarm, and neither cold nor hot, I will spew thee out of my mouth.

[17] Because thou sayest, I am rich, and increased with goods, and have need of nothing; and knowest not that thou art wretched, and miserable, and poor, and blind, and naked:

[18] I counsel thee to buy of me gold tried in the fire, that thou mayest be rich; and white raiment, that thou mayest be clothed, and that the shame of thy nakedness do not appear; and anoint thine eyes with eyesalve, that thou mayest see.

[19] As many as I love, I rebuke and chasten: be zealous therefore, and repent.

[20] Behold, I stand at the door, and knock: if any man hear my voice, and open the door, I will come in to him, and will sup with him, and he with me.

[21] To him that overcometh will I grant to sit with me in my throne, even as I also overcame, and am set down with my Father in his throne.

[22] He that hath an ear, let him hear what the Spirit saith unto the churches.

Purchase   Bishop's   Books   @
www.lulu.com/amoslhorton

Email:

amoshortonministry@gmail.com

Web:
www.amoshortonministries.org

This is the beginning of many books to come as mentioned in the table of Contents

If you desire to book bishop Horton for speaking engagements feel free to request him. The information is below

bookingbishop@angelic.com
amoshortonministry@gmail.com

Thank you and God bless you

www.ingramcontent.com/pod-product-compliance
Lightning Source LLC
Chambersburg PA
CBHW032018090426

42741CB00006B/652